RUNIC EVOLUTION & LINGUISTIC HISTORY (BLACK & WHITE VERSION)

The Origin Of The Germanic Runes & Universal Rune Sets

All Natural Spirit

CONTENTS

PREFACE

Within the world of runic literature there exists a very clear divide between the academic runologists and the new age diviners. I hope that with this book, and its follow-up counter parts, I can provide a bridge between the two perspectives regarding the study and use of the runic alphabets.

I have been researching the runic alphabets extensively for the last few years and they have become a prominent feature on my website (www.allnaturalspirit.com). They have been a source of inspiration for several scholarly articles and have been distilled into oracle decks, print-on-demand art and now an entire book series! My fascination with this ancient writing script seems far from spent as I constantly develop innovative techniques and products to utilize the runes to gain wisdoms from the collective consciousness as well as the depth of our own souls.

My initial and primary objective was to create a trust-worthy, 'universal' representative of each of the Runic Alphabets, backed-up by proper research that can be used as divinatory tools. My use of the word 'divinatory' does not mean fortune telling or predictions of the future. Rather the use of the divination here is to acts as a communication method with your higher consciousness to facilitate self-development and spiritual growth. In order to identify this illusive universal rune sets I had to start from the very beginning, the linguistic origins of the runes.

This was quite an undertaking – I remember being thoroughly confused at the discombobulated state of Runic literature and I went through heaps of literature to find the handful of informative ones I used for the reconstructions illustrated in this book.

I believe that I have managed to create a standard set of runes for each of the Elder Futhark, Anglo-Saxon Futhorc and Younger Futhork with justification for some of the rune scripts favored above others as per scholarly debate. Having this proper foundation leads to a more creative endeavor, the construction of the Bindrunes – of which endless combinations can be made for a multitude of purposes!

LIST OF BOOKS IN THIS SERIES

Runes Book 2: *Celestial Rune Sigils: Elder Futhark BindRunes* by All Natural Spirit (2020).

Runes Book 3: *Elder Futhark Arcanum: An Intuitive Interpretation of Rune Meanings* by All Natural Spirit (2021)

For more information, please see the Books in this Series section at the end of the book.

* * *

INTRODUCTION

We start our runic journey with the rune linguistic origins of the Elder Futhark, Anglo-Saxon Futhorc and Younger Futhark. We also explore how these three ancient alphabets relate to one another and the other alphabets during the same time. Afterwards we head on to brief overviews of each of the runic alphabet sets and how I came to choose the letter, rune script and names for each based on the most prominent and trustworthy information from hard-to-find expert runologist and runology sources. I grouped the discussions around the basic alphabet structure, the sorting of conflicting rune meanings and the diversity of runic symbols in some sets. Lastly, I end the book of with a brief description of bindrunes, which leads me to introduce the next book I am currently working on.

* * *

WHAT ARE THE RUNES?

Strictly speaking; the runes collectively represent the earliest of alphabets and primitive writing systems, such that letters can be easily carved into wood or stone using a blade or mallet and chisel.

There are many different linguistic origins for the first alphabets including Celtic, Italic (now Roman), Hellenic (now Greek) and Germanic. This is covered in detail in the next chapter. As mentioned previously, this book will focus on the runes of Germanic origin, such as the Elder Futhark, Anglo Saxon Futhorc and Younger Futhark each discussed in their separate chapters.

The most interesting aspect of the runes is their modern use in divinatory and magickal rituals. Here the rituals refer to a set of steps through which you facilitate self-development, such as the burning of candles or incense while meditation – setting the spiritual mood as it were. Bindrunes play a very important role in the magickal aspect of bindrunes and are a doorway to practicing creativity and problem solving.

* * *

LINGUISTIC HISTORY OF THE RUNES

The Runic alphabets lack standardization, mostly due to the way in which each originated from the predecessor and several influences from the Roman language and its scriptures. For instance, when you simply type 'Runes' into a search engine you would find contradictions between the available sets – all of which are denoted as the 'correct' version. Doubting many of these sources, I began pulling information from more credible expert sources, specifically those from scholarly Runologists (not just the new age books).

In this chapter I would like to illustrate the linguistic flow of the runes and how that gave rise to the other rune systems as well as explaining the potential discrepancies between available literatures. Thus, we will start with the overview of how the systems originated and then how they co-evolved from the most primitive of languages.

The runic alphabet along with the Latin alphabet is generally believed to be derived from Old Italic (with additional influence by Greek, Latin and Etruscan) as part of the Indo-European languages (Figure 1). The term 'rune' is used to describe an alphabet and/or writing system other than that of Latin or Greek letters. These are generally angular in shape as they were primarily used for inscribing wood and/or carving stone.

The root for Rune is:

- 'run' in Germanic and 'runs' in Gothic, both inclining to the words: secret or whisper

- 'runo' in Proto-Germanic (primitive Germanic) that means letter, literature or secret

Figure 1: A map of the geographical distribution of the Indo-European languages.

When we look at the original languages of the Indo-Europeans we can determine the linguistic origins of each of the runes. For simplicity, we start with the 'original' languages; each is a separate language and is distinct from the other (Figure 2, Top line). Here we have Hellenic, Italic, Celtic and Germanic making up the 'top-tier' of the linguistic evolutionary tree if you will. Thereafter, we see each develop through history due to the spread of the tribes, their inevitable convergence and how this influenced and moulded the present-day forms.

I am mainly concerned with the Germanic languages, but I will provide a quick summary regarding the language association for each of the original languages:

- Hellenic → Greek

- Italic → Latin/Roman

- Celtic → Irish

- Germanic → Norse, Frisian, English, Saxon and Gothic

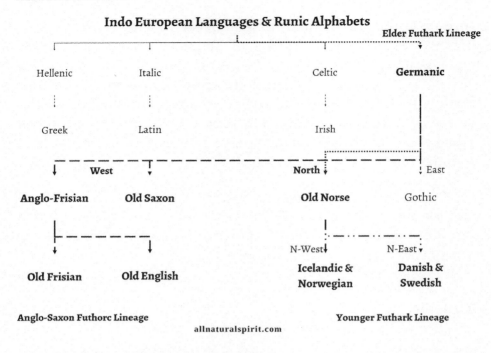

Figure 2: A flow diagram indicating the Indo-European languages of the tribes and the development of the runic alphabets. Possible Elder Futhark lineage (linguistic evolution) in Dots, Younger Futhark lineage in Long-Dash-Double-Dots and Anglo-Saxon Futhorc lineage in Long-Dash.

From the picture above, I have indicated the flow of the Germanic languages, depending on the locations of the various tribes during that time. 'Northern Germanic' (Long-Dash-Double-Dots) developed into Old Norse, followed by Icelandic/Norwegian in the 'North'-West and Danish/Swedish in the 'North'-East. 'Eastern Germanic' gave rise to a single Gothic system, whereas the 'Western Germanic' (Long Dash) split-off into Anglo-Frisian and Old-Saxon. The Anglo-Saxon lineage then gave rise to Old Frisian and Old English. Subsequently, we have covered the necessary background information required to discuss the development of the alphabets for each of the languages.

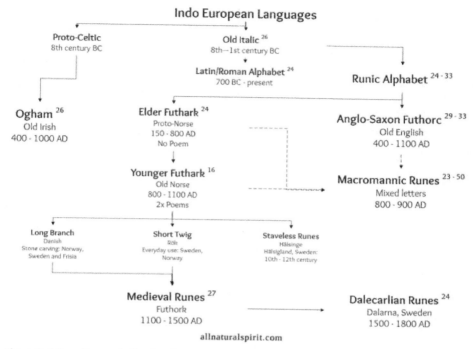

Figure 3: A flow diagram indication the evolution of the Runic Alphabets over the centuries. Super-scripts indicate the number of letters in each system. Language and location associations are also listed. Superscripts indicate the number of runes in each alphabet, some indicate a range of values which include additional rune variants.

During the initiation of Indo-European languages it would seem that Old Italic and Proto-Celtic were present at somewhat the same time (~ 800 BC). The Latin or Roman alphabet was derived from Old Italic (~ 700 BC) and has been in use to this present day as the main working alphabet, which we are all very familiar with. Initially, we see that the Runic Alphabets split off from Old Italic and they develop in isolation from the Roman language and its counterparts for a few centuries. At this point in time we are already a bit farther down the linguistic lineage, hence we see the influence of Old Italic on the Runic Alphabets. In contrast, some scholars argue that the Runic Alphabets are derived from the Roman one...

When Proto-Germanic dominated during 150-800 AD, we predominantly find the Elder Futhark amongst the few surviving carvings. The letters of the Elder Futhark are clear and very few variants exist, giving rise to a mostly coherent system of runes. Very little is known about the pronunciation and meaning of the Proto-Germanic letters, since there is no 'Proto-Germanic Poem' or 'Runic Poem' equivalent for the Elder Futhark as for the Anglo-Saxon Futhorc and Younger Futhark. Thus, the rune names are derived from Proto-Germanic approximations and their meanings are retro-fitted from the Anglo-Saxon rune poem. I provide a quick summary for the Elder Futhark system for reference (Figure 4). A comprehensive overview of the Elder Futhark is provided in the following chapter.

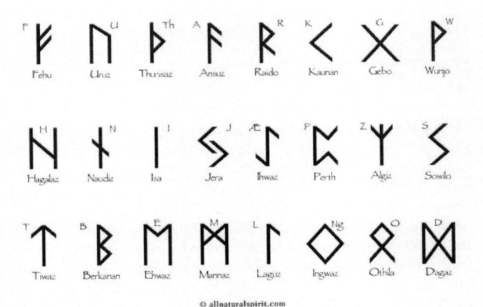

© allnaturalspirit.com

Figure 4: An illustration of the universal Elder Futhark rune set as elucidated from runologic research. The mini oracle deck based on these cards are available from my MakePlayingCards On-line Store, details of which are available on my website.

While the Elder Futhark was still in use (150-800 AD), we see the expanded Anglo-Saxon Futhorc (400-1100 AD) arise with several similarities to the Elder Futhark. However, this runic alphabet is a Futhorc due to the linguistic and pronunciation changes between Proto-Germanic and Anglo-Saxon. Before we move on, I provide a similar summary picture for the Anglo-Saxon Futhorc.

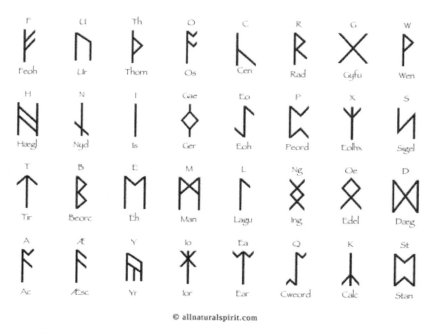

© allnaturalspirit.com

Figure 5: An illustration of the universal Anglo-Saxon Futhorc rune set as elucidated from runologic research. The mini oracle deck based on these cards are available from my MakePlayingCards Online Store, details of which are available on my website.

The Elder Futhark and Anglo-Saxon Futhorc systems co-existed for some time and later when Proto-Germanic becomes Proto-Norse then Old-Norse we see the Elder Futhark being completely replaced by a reduced Younger Futhark (technically it should be an Younger Futhork by linguistic standards...). The Younger Futhark co-exists with the Anglo-Saxon Futhorc for some time as well. One can almost view the Elder Futhark runes as the 'older sister' system of the Anglo-Saxon runes, whereas the Younger Fu-thark is the 'daughter system' of the Elder Futhark (i.e., replacing the previous version). Furthermore, we see the Younger Futhark split-off into 3 different variants over the centuries, hence the reason for 2 different Younger Futhark rune poems! This is where things get messy, real messy! Before we move on, I provide a similar summary picture for the Younger Futhark, specifically the more widely used Danish/Icelandic version.

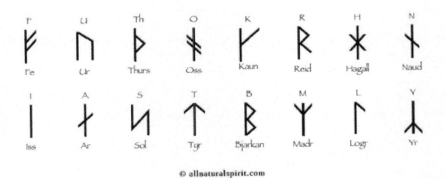

© allnaturalspirit.com

Figure 6: An illustration of the universal Younger Futhark rune set as elucidated from runologic research. The mini oracle deck based on these cards are available from my MakePlayingCards Online Store, details of which are available on my website.

Because of the centuries-long overlap between the three systems, there was a lot of mixing-and-matching going on. Combinations of the three systems are known as the Macromannic Runes. The Younger Futhark was easier to piece together as it was generally left alone. However, the Anglo-Saxon runes experienced even more expansion due to the influence from religious missionaries and other scholars who tried to correlate the Runic alphabet with the Roman one. So you see all kinds of fanciful things on carvings and in recorded scriptures during this time, not to mention the catastrophic loss of ancient books in library fires, which may have held the key to solving this massive runic mix-up! We also may even notice some influence on the runes from the Ogham (or Celtic Script 400-1000 AD). The Ogham is a whole different research project on its own! Thus, we return to the runic confusion.

Phew! My head was practically spinning at this stage, but with some tables (provided in the next chapters) I managed to elucidate a potential standardised set of runes for each of the Elder Futhark, Anglo-Saxon Futhorc and Younger Futhark, which have subsequently been made into Mini-Oracle decks. Moving on with the runic evolutionary ladder...

Macromanic Runes
Southern Carolingian Empire
Alemannia, Bavaria
800 - 900 AD

a	Asch	⟨runes⟩	i	His	⟨rune⟩	r	Rehit	⟨runes⟩
b	Birith	⟨runes⟩	k	Gilch	⟨runes⟩	s	Suhil	⟨runes⟩
ch	Khen	⟨runes⟩	l	Lagu	⟨rune⟩	t	Tac	⟨rune⟩
th	Thorn	⟨runes⟩	m	Man	⟨rune⟩	u	Hur	⟨runes⟩
e	Eho	⟨rune⟩	n	Not	⟨runes⟩	x	Helahe	⟨runes⟩
f	Fehc	⟨runes⟩	o	Othil	⟨runes⟩	y	Huyri	⟨runes⟩
g	Gibu	⟨runes⟩	p	Perch	⟨runes⟩	z	Ziu	⟨runes⟩
h	Hagele	⟨runes⟩	q	Khon	⟨rune⟩			

Figure 7: An illustration of sketched Macromannic Runes.

11

The Younger Futhark and Anglo-Saxon Futhorc fell out of use at round-about the same time. Then we see another set of Runes arise, derived from an expanded Younger Futhark system, known as the Medieval Runes (1100-1500 AD, also a Futhork by linguistic accounts). These very much retain that mixy-matchy feeling of the runic alphabet evolution at this time, with several influences from the Roman, Celtic and maybe even Gothic systems. The runes are slowly being replaced by the more prominent and well-developed Greek and Roman systems. A final 'speciation' event of the runes occurred with the development of the Dalecarlian Runes (1500-1800 AD). You would notice a very strong influence from the Roman alphabet as the Runic alphabet tries to stubbornly hold on, but slowly gives way to the 'superior' of the two systems. Although, some variants of these runes are still in use today it has mostly become an extinct system of writing.

Medieval Runes
Futhork
1100 - 1500 AD

Dalecarlian Runes
Dalarna, Sweden
1500 - 1800 AD

Figure 8: An illustration of sketched Medieval and Dalecarlian runes.

That concludes the evolutionary journey into the ancient past of the Runic Alphabets. As mentioned before I will discuss each of the Rune systems (Elder Futhark, Younger Futhark and Anglo-Saxon) in the coming chapters. I will also give some background information to their potential use in divination and metaphysical connotations.

* * *

ELDER FUTHARK OVERVIEW

- Oldest Runic Alphabet (150-800 AD)
- Writing System for the Germanic tribes and Northwest Germanic dialects
- A set of 24 letters
- Full alphabet first discovered on the Kylver Stone, Gotland, 400 AD

Figure 9: A sketch of the Kylver runestone from Gotland, Sweden (1934) including an enlarged ver-
ion of the runes carved on the stone.

Elder Futhark Origin

T he parent language or linguistic origin of the Elder Futh-ark is highly debated and could have arisen from Latin, Greek or Etruscan. There is also indication that the Elder Futhark is derived from the Semitic-Arabic writings dating from the Bronze Age and the early Iron Age in the Near East. This Semitic origin places the Elder Futhark in the time frame of 2000-1000 BC, which indicates that it may even be older than the Greek alphabet (750 BC)! The evidence the author provides for this becomes highly technical from a linguistic, writing and pronunciation aspect, but it simply stems from the fact that both the Elder Futhark and Greek language share traits of the previ-ous ancestral language rather than the Elder Futhark only sharing similarities to the 'later' Greek language, which would have been the case should it have arisen from the Greek language instead of the more ancestral one.

The Elder Futhark is a set of 24 Germanic alphabet discovered in Gotland (1903) on the Kylver Stone that dates back to 400 AD. They represent one of the earliest writing scripts. It is postulated that they were inspired by the natural surroundings and life his-tories of the people during that time. The exact script usage and meaning of each has been lost to time and the Old English Rune Poem has been used as an improvisation for the rune meanings.

The Old English Rune Poem is of Anglo-Saxon origin and dates well after the Elder Futhark. The Rune Poem is dated to the 8th and 9th century, whereas the Elder Futhark dates from 2nd to 8th century. Therefore, the Elder Futhark and the Rune Poem aren't clearly linked and there is much scholarly debate as to the translation of both the script and the poem. The Rune Poem, especially, had been copied multiple times by hand from historic manuscripts that have been lost in library fires (a very common phenomenon in the past) and subsequently no "original" version exists. Here copying error and translation errors could have crept in during (re)documentation. As such the both the translation and interpretation of the Rune Poem is very subjective. I believe it is best for you to acquire a translation version of the poem that resonates with you and to interpret its exact meaning for yourself should you wish to use the runes for divinatory purposes.

Elder Futhark Alphabet Division and Use

The Elder Futhark is divided into 3 Aetts or 'families', representing a set of 8 runes in each. There is vague epigraphic (the study of inscriptions as writing) reference from 2 bracteates, specifically the Grumpan and Vadstena bracteates (Figure 10), for this division. Modern metaphysicians specialising in rune research claim that this division represents three gods from Norse mythology, namely Freyja (the warrior goddess), Heimdallr (the god of visions) and Tyr (the god of victory). However, the Elder Futhark is Proto-Germanic, a very ancient language from which Old Norse arose as well as several other languages, such as Anglo-Frisian and Old Saxon. Thus, the Elder Futhark very much pre-dates the Old Norse gods. Some Old Norse references exist that discuss the god Tiwaz, the Proto-Germanic version of Tyr. Thus, this 'modern reason' for the division of the Elder Futhark into Aetts is poorly supported, due to the lack of Proto-Germanic scriptures existing today. This does not mean that you cannot use the Old Norse divisions for your metaphysical practises; it simply indicates lack of historic evidence. Although, absence of evidence is not evidence of absence, yet it remains somewhat doubtful that the Old Norse gods are the reason. This stems from the debate surrounding the original use of the Elder Futhark, which was for writing and not divination. The use of the Elder Futhark as a divinatory tool only came later after the Elder Futhark fell out of use for writing and when the Roman alphabet became more prominent. This created a certain 'mystical allure' surrounding the ancient runic alphabets and it became more popular to use as a magical tool. Thus, the reason for the Elder Futhark families remains largely unknown.

Figure 10: A sketch of the Vadstena bracteate (500 AD) is a gold C-bracteate or gold sheet found in the earth at Vadstena, Sweden in 1774. The bracteate is famous for containing a full listing of the Elder Futhark Runic alphabet. The runes in the futhark are divided by dots into three groups of eight runes which are commonly called an ætt. The bracteate was stolen in 1938 from the Swedish Museum of National Antiquities and has not yet been found.

Elder Futhark Alphabet Structure

T he Elder Futhark is made up of 24 letters, it is the oldest of the runic alphabets and its namesake is also derived from the sound values of its first 6 letters as written on the Kylver stone, i.e., "F U TH A R K" (Figure 9). There are approximately 250 inscriptions of the Elder Futhark distributed between Denmark, Norway, Sweden, Germany, Frisia and England. By comparing all these to find most common elements, you would have the following alphabet:

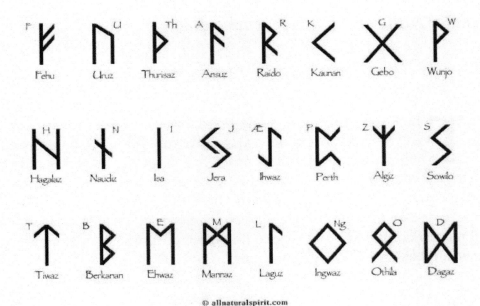

Figure 11: An illustration of the universal Elder Futhark rune set as elucidated from runologic research. The mini oracle deck based on these cards are available from my MakePlayingCards On-line Store, details of which are available on my website.

Generally the rune shape, letters and even pronunciation are well defined and consistent. Note that 'th' is translated from the sound Þ, æ roughly comes from ï, whereas the z letter is pronounced as a palatal r in Scandinavian/Icelandic (written as ʀ) and 'ng' comes from ŋ.

Elder Futhark Alphabet Meanings

The meaning of each letter is connected to animals, plants and events related to the people and livelihoods of that time. Unlike the basic structure, many inconsistencies arise from the meaning of each of these letters, which are generally derived from the Old English Rune Poem which is of Anglo-Saxon origin. This represents a retro-fitting of Old English onto Proto-Germanic (skipping over Proto-Norse and Old Norse between the languages as they developed). Thus, the meaning of the Elder Futhark is somewhat obscure and depending on which runologist or Proto-Germanic interpretation you refer to, the letters may have different meanings - because language is not static and one word can have multiple sometimes unrelated meanings. I have searched for all the common alphabet meanings and their variants, which you use for your metaphysical practise is up to you.

Figure 12: A scan of the Old English or Anglo-Saxon Rune Poem by G. Hickes (1703). Source: Dbach-mann, Wikipedia.

Elder Futhark Conclusion

After working through the runic literature I have created the following table below, it represents the most common Proto-Germanic writing and name, the English transliteration and potential meanings associated with these.

Table 1: Elder Futhark Rune symbols, names, transliterations and meanings. Reconstructed from the consensus between several references (see Top 10 Inforamtive References chapter) to represent a potential universal set of runes.

#	Proto-Norse Writing	Proto-Germanic Name	English Transliteration	Conventional Meaning†
1	ᚠ	fehu	f	cattle/wealth
2	ᚢ	uruz	u	auroch/wild ox
3	ᚦ	thurisaz	þ (th)	giant
4	ᚨ	ansuz	a	mouth/messenger
5	ᚱ	raido	r	ride/riding
6	ᚲ	kaunan	c	ulcer/torch
7	ᚷ	gebo	g	gift
8	ᚹ	wunjo	w	joy
9	ᚺ	hagalaz	h	hail (precipitation)
10	ᚾ	naudiz	n	need
11	ᛁ	isa	i	ice
12	ᛃ	jera	j	year/harvest
13	ᛇ	ihwaz	æ	yew tree
14	ᛈ	perth	p	pear tree/dice cup
15	ᛉ	algiz	z	elk/sedge
16	ᛊ	sowilo	s	sun
17	ᛏ	tiwaz	t	god Tyr/Tiw
18	ᛒ	berkanan	b	birch tree
19	ᛖ	ehwaz	e	horse
20	ᛗ	mannaz	m	man
21	ᛚ	laguz	l	lake
22	ᛜ	ingwaz	ing	god Yngvi/Ing
23	ᛟ	othila	o	heritage/property/estate
24	ᛞ	dagaz	d	day

© allnaturalspirit.com
† Approximated from Anglo-Saxon rune poem (i.e., nobody knows for sure!)
* A downloadable PDF version of the table is available from my website to go along with the Deck @ https://allnaturalspirit.files.wordpress.com/2020/08/elder-futhark-summary-1.pdf

I would recommend that you learn all the meanings and allow the surrounding runes from your rune cast to distinguish which meaning would be more appropriate for the given reading. After all reading oracles from runes requires a bit of creativity and intuitive interpretation from your side.

�֍ �֍ ✖

ANGLO-SAXON FUTHORC OVERVIEW

- Second Oldest Runic Alphabet (400-1100 AD)
- Derived from the Older Elder Futhark
- Writing System for the Anglo-Saxon dialects (Anglo-Frisian, Old Saxon, Old Frisian and Old English)
- A set of 33 letters
- Anglo-Saxon or Anglo-Frisian Poem (8-9th century) as reference point for the letters and their potential meanings.

Figure 13: A sketch of the Anglo-Saxon futhorc (*abecedarium anguliscum*) as presented in Codex Sangallensis 878 (9th century).

Anglo-Saxon Futhorc Origin and Expansion

T he sister language and/or linguistic influence of the Anglo-Saxon Futhorc is the Elder Futhark, which is a Proto Germanic runic alphabet. The Elder Futhark (400 - 800 AD) existed prior to the Anglo-Saxon Futhorc and both co-existed for some time (300 years). During this time; new languages arose between the tribes, such as Anglo-Frisian, Old Saxon, Old Frisian and Old English.

Due to changes in linguistic pronunciation and writing from Proto/Old Norse to Old English the Anglo-Saxon Futhorc almost seems to shift the Elder Futhark alphabetical order as well as introducing several new alphabet letters. This includes the switching, mixing and trading of original Elder Futhark letters, known as a linguistic chain shift. Notice not only the change in the writing symbols, but also the change in pronunciation, especially considering the vowels.

For example:

- **Letter 3;** Ansuz become Os: a → o
- **Letter 13;** Ihwaz becomes Eoh: æ → eo
- **Letter 23;** Othila becomes Edel: o → eo

Furthermore, you observe the Christian and Roman missionaries interact with the Germanic tribes during this time. These religious scholars were prompted to attempt to align the Roman and Anglo-Saxon alphabets, because of the language/alphabet barrier between the Latin speaking and Anglo-Saxon speaking people. This heavily influenced the 'language evolution' of the Anglo-Saxon Futhorc, a process is known as the Anglo-Saxon Christianization. During this dynamic expansion of the Anglo-Saxon Futhorc you see it increase from the 24 Elder Futhark letters to 26, later 28/29 and finally 33 letters. Thus, one finds a multitude of different Anglo-Saxon variants as well as somewhat familiar looking letters to our own alphabet within this Futhorc.

Anglo-Saxon Futhorc Alphabet Structure

The final set of Anglo-Saxon Fuhorc runes is made up of 33 letters. Similar to the Elder Futhark, its namesake is also derived from the sound values of its first 6 letters, i.e., "FU THORC". Due to the vowel changes pointed out previously, the "F U THARK" became "FU THORC".

The Anglo-Saxon Rune Poem or Old English Rune Poem plays a pivotal role in the structure, lettering and meaning of the Anglo-Saxon runes. It provides meaning to each rune through stanzas, a grouped set of lines within a poem, which may or may not rhyme. However, there is much scholarly debate as to the translation of the poem and stanzas only exist for the first 29 of the 33 letters.

The first edition of the Rune Poem was contained in a historical manuscript, the *Linguarum veterum septentrionalium thesaurus grammatico-criticus et archæologicus* by George Hickes during 1703. The original manuscript (MS Cotton Otho B. X) perished in the Cottonian library fire of 1731, thus George Hickes' edition became the only copy of the Rune Poem (Figure 14).

allnaturalspirit.com

Figure 14: A scan of the Old English or Anglo-Saxon Rune Poem by G. Hickes (1703). Source: Dbach-mann, Wikipedia.

Anglo-Saxon or Old English Rune Poem

Similarities of the Thesaurus to the MS Cotton Domitian A. IX sparked scholarly debate as to whether the Rune Poem was even recorded in the original perished manuscript. Investigation into the inconsistencies between the old manuscripts revealed additional oddities, due to hand-copying, translation efforts and comparisons of the Elder Futhark with the reduced Younger Futhark (9th century, Scandinavian origin, 16 runes) and expanded Futhorc (5th century, Anglo-Saxon or Anglo-Frisian origin, 33 runes). Therefore, it is postulated that both copying error and translation errors could have crept into the (re)documented versions of the Rune Poem. As such both the translations and interpretation of the Rune Poem is very subjective and should be used with consideration.

Further difficulties of establishing a universal rune set for the Anglo-Saxon Futhorc is caused by the up to 39 variants of the 33 runes. However, the Domitian A. IX and the Galba A. I manuscripts have the closest runic similarities to the poem and to one another. Up to 28 runes from the Domitian A. IX version occur in more than 70% of other Anglo-Saxon rune material and 27 of these appear in the poem. Therefore, by comparing several different Anglo-Saxon variants and tracking the linguistic changes as described by runologists and linguists to find most common elements, you would have the following alphabet:

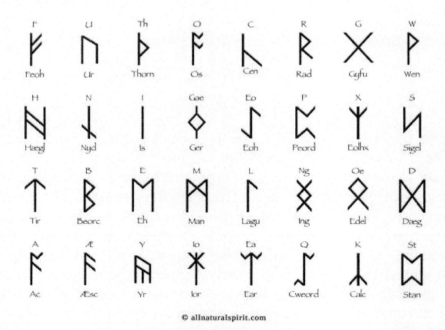

© allnaturalspirit.com

Figure 15: An illustration of the universal Anglo-Saxon Futhorc rune set as elucidated from runo-logic research. The mini oracle deck based on these cards are available from my MakePlayingCards Online Store, details of which are available on my website.

Here the Anglo-Saxon Futhorc has variants of all 24 Elder Futhark letters, an additional 5 vowels (Ac, Æsc, Yr, Ior and Ear) and 4 new letters (Cweord, Calc, Stan and Gar).

Anglo-Saxon Futhorc Alphabet Meanings

T he meaning of each letter is connected to animals, plants and events related to the people and livelihoods of that time. As mentioned before, many inconsistencies arise from the meaning of each of these letters, which are generally derived from the Old English Rune Poem which is of Anglo-Saxon origin, but it only provides meanings for the first 29 runes. The exact meaning of the runes are subjective depending on which English translation of the poem you refer to. Therefore, each letter may have different meanings - because language is not static and one word can have multiple sometimes unrelated meanings, which you use for your metaphysical practise is up to you.

Anglo-Saxon Futhorc Conclusion

After working through the runic literature I have created the following table below, it represents the most common Anglo-Saxon writing and name, the English transliteration as well as a comparison with the original Elder Futhark associated with of the letters.

Table 2: Anglo-Saxon Rune symbols, names, transliterations and meanings. Reconstructed from the consensus between several references (see Top 10 Inforamtive References chapter) to represent a potential universal set of runes.

#	Elder Futhark	Anglo-Saxon	Anglo-Saxon Name	English Transliteration
1	ᚠ	ᚠ	feoh	f
2	ᚢ	ᚢ	ur	u
3	ᚦ	ᚦ	thorn	þ (th)
4	ᚨ	ᚩ	os	o [replaces a]
5	ᚱ	ᚱ	rad	r
6	ᚲ	ᚳ	cen	c
7	ᚷ	ᚷ	gyfu	g
8	ᚹ	ᚹ	wen	w
9	ᚺ	ᚻ	hægl	h
10	ᚾ	ᚾ	nyd	n
11	ᛁ	ᛁ	is	i
12	ᛃ	ᛄ	ger	gae [replaces j]
13	ᛇ	ᛇ	eoh	eo [replaces æ]
14	ᛈ	ᛈ	perod	p
15	ᛉ	ᛉ	eolhx	x [replaces z]
16	ᛋ	ᛋ	sigel	s
17	ᛏ	ᛏ	tir	t
18	ᛒ	ᛒ	beorc	b
19	ᛖ	ᛖ	eh	e
20	ᛗ	ᛗ	man	m
21	ᛚ	ᛚ	lagu	l
22	ᛜ	ᛝ	ing	ng [replaces ing]
23	ᛟ	ᛟ	edel	oe [replaces o]
24	ᛞ	ᛞ	dæg	d
25	-	ᚪ	ac	a
26	-	ᚫ	Æsc	æ
27	-	ᚣ	yr	y
28	-	ᛡ	ior	io
29	-	ᛠ	ear	ea
30	-	ᚳ	cweorth	q
31	-	ᛣ	calc	k
32	-	ᛢ	stan	st
33	-	ᚸ	gar	g [additional g]

* A downloadable PDF version of the table is available from my website to go along with the Deck @ https://allnaturalspirit.files.wordpress.com/2020/08/anglo-saxon-futhorc-summary-1.pdf

I have not added the meanings to the table as they are even more variable that the alphabet structure including some entirely missing meanings. I believe it is best for anyone interested in learning this system to acquire a translated version of the Rune

Poem, which resonates with you and to interpret its exact meaning for yourself. You can use the 'traditional' interpretations as a rough guide (such as those in Ref 4 from the Top 10 Informative References chapter are a good starting point), but you will find that some of your own interpretations start to deviate from the widely used norm. I would also recommend that you learn all the meanings and allow the surrounding runes from your rune cast to distinguish which meaning would be more appropriate for the given reading. After all, reading oracles from runes requires a bit of creativity and intuitive interpretation from your side.

* * *

YOUNGER FUTHARK OVERVIEW

- Third Oldest Runic Alphabet (800-1100 AD)
- Direct descendant of the Germanic Elder Futhark
- Writing System for the Old West Norse (Old Icelandic, Old Norwegian and Greenlandic Norse) and Old East Norse dialects (Old Danish, Old Swedish and Old Gutnish)
- A set of 16 letters
- 2x Younger Futhark Poems; namely the Icelandic (13th century) and Norwegian (15th century) as reference point for the letters and their potential meanings.

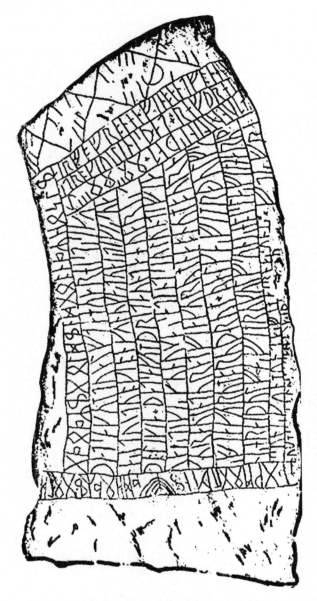

Figure 16: A sketch of the Rökstenen, the longest Younger Futhark runestone inscription in the world, Near Ödeshög in south Sweden.

Younger Futhark Origin and Expansion

An Old Norse daughter system with a direct linguistic inheritance from the Elder Futhark, which is a Proto Germanic runic alphabet. The Elder Futhark (400 - 800 AD) existed prior to the Younger Futhark (800 - 1100 AD), which overlaps 300 years with the Anglo-Saxon Futhorc (400 - 1100 AD) time frame. During this time; new languages arose between the Old Norse or Scandinavian tribes, such as Old Icelandic, Old Norwegian, Old Danish and Old Swedish.

Due to changes in linguistic pronunciation and writing from Proto-Germanic then Proto-Norse to Old Norse the Younger Futhark reduces the number of Elder Futhark letters from 24 to 16 by merging several vowels and/or consonants. There are also vowel changes, due to the difference in pronunciation between Proto-Norse to Old Norse, known as a linguistic chain shift. Notice not only the change in the writing symbols, but also the change in pronunciation, especially considering the vowels.

For example:

- **Letter 3;** Ansuz becomes Oss: a → o
- **Letter 12 and 13;** Jera + Ihwaz seem to merge to Ar: j/ae → a
- **Letter 15;** Algiz becomes Yr: z → y

The Younger Futhark has a bit more variation than the parental Elder Futhark system, however is far more consistent than the Anglo-Saxon Futhorc.

Younger Futhark Alphabet Structure

T he final set of Younger Futhark runes is made up of 16 letters. It inherits its namesake from the Elder Futhark. However, should you also apply the same logic and derive its namesake from the sound values of its first 6 letters such as done for the Elder Futhark, i.e., "F U TH A R K" you would notice that due to the vowel changes pointed out previously, the "F U TH A R K" should actually be "F U TH O R K", hence Younger Futhork.

The alphabet structure of the Younger Futhark not only changed due to pronunciation changes, but also the materials used to carve the letters. One rune represented more than one sound and, thus the shape simplified.

There Are Three Versions Of The Younger Futhark (Figure 17):

- **Long Branch** (Danish), 8th century and dominant in all areas of Denmark until the 10th century - **This is the one I used for the Deck**
- **Short Twig** (Swedish and Norwegian), 8th century and primarily used in Sweden and Norway
- **Hälsinge** (Staveless), 10th century and used for a short period in the Hälsingland region of Sweden

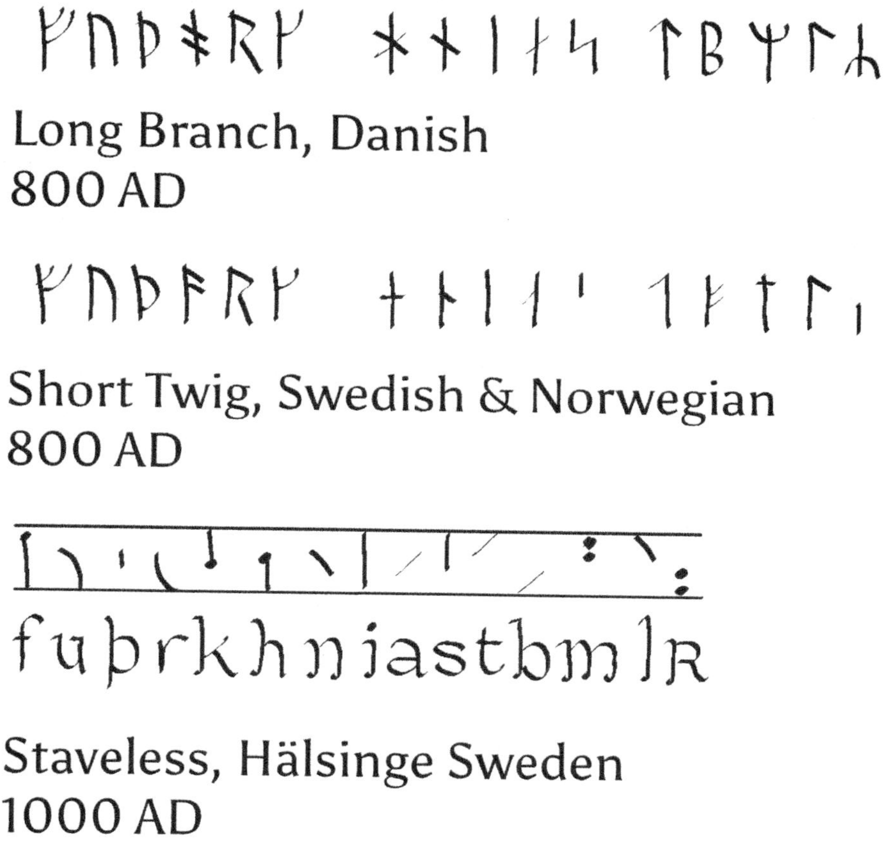

ᚠᚢᚦᚬᚱᚴ ᚼᚾᛁᛏᛅ ᛏᛒᛘᛚᛦ

Long Branch, Danish
800 AD

ᚠᚢᚦ�009ᚱᚴ ᛏᚽᛁᛁ' ᛁᚽᛏᚱᛁ

Short Twig, Swedish & Norwegian
800 AD

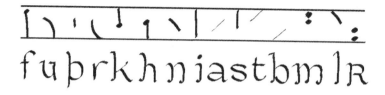

fuþrkhnjastbmlʀ

Staveless, Hälsinge Sweden
1000 AD

Figure 17: An illustration of the different variants of sketched Younger Futhark runes.

Similar to the Anglo-Saxon Futhorc, the Younger Futhark also has runic poems (Icelandic and Norwegian). The Icelandic poem is the most concise and oldest of the two, whereas the Norwegian version available today is a copy from a destroyed manuscript - which may have been prone to translation/copy error.

The Icelandic Rune Poem plays a pivotal role in the structure, lettering and meaning of the Younger Futhark runes. It provides meaning to each rune through stanzas, a grouped set of lines within a poem, which may or may not rhyme. The Icelandic Rune Poem is recorded in four *Arnamagnæan* manuscripts (15th century). Considering that Old Icelandic is far easier to translate than Old Norse or Old English, the poem should be considered fairly representative of the Younger Futhark runes - there may be slight variation dependent on who translates the piece.

Therefore, by comparing several different old manuscript recordings, such as the *Arnamagnæan* and *Runologia* (1778), of the linguistic changes as described by runologists and linguists to find most common elements, you would have the following alphabet:

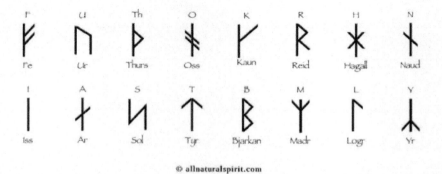

© allnaturalspirit.com

Figure 18: An illustration of the universal Younger Futhark rune set as elucidated from runologic research. The mini oracle deck based on these cards are available from my MakePlayingCards Online Store, details of which are available on my website.

Here the Younger Futhark has reduced variants of the 24 Elder Futhark letters.

Younger Futhark Alphabet Meanings

The meaning of each letter is connected to animals, plants and events related to the people and livelihoods of that time. As mentioned before, the most representative source for these meanings is the Icelandic Rune Poem and many translations are available on the internet.

Younger Futhark Conclusion

After working through the runic literature I have created the following table below, it represents the most common Younger Futhark writing and name, the English transliteration as well as a comparison with the original Elder Futhark associated with of the letters. This final table concludes our journey into the evolution and linguistic history of the runic alphabets.

Table 3: Younger Futhark Rune symbols, names, transliterations and meanings. Reconstructed from the consensus between several references (see Top 10 Informative References chapter) to represent a potential universal set of runes.

#	Elder Futhark	Younger Futhark	Icelandic Name✝	English Transliteration✝
1	ᚠ	ᚠ	fe	f
2	ᚢ	ᚢ	ur	u
3	ᚦ	ᚦ	thurs	þ (th)
4	ᚨ	ᚬ	oss	o
5	ᚱ	ᚱ	reid	r
6	ᚲ	ᚴ	kaun	k
7	ᚷ	-	-	-
8	ᚹ	-	-	-
9	ᚺ	ᚼ	hagall	h
10	ᚾ	ᚾ	naud	n
11	ᛁ	ᛁ	iss	i
12	ᛃ	ᛅ	ar	a
13	ᛇ	-	-	-
14	ᛈ	-	-	-
15	ᛉ	ᛘ	yr	y [moves to end]
16	ᛊ	ᛋ	sol	s
17	ᛏ	ᛏ	tyr	t
18	ᛒ	ᛒ	bjarkan	b
19	ᛖ	-	-	-
20	ᛗ	ᛉ	madr	m
21	ᛚ	ᛚ	logr	l
22	ᛜ	-	-	-
23	ᛟ	-	-	-
24	ᛞ	-	-	-

© allnaturalspirit.com

✝ Directly from R. I. Page translations

* A downloadable PDF version of the table (https://allnaturalspirit.files.wordpress.com/2020/08/younger-futhark-summary-1.pdf) as well as a translation of the Icelandic Rune Poem (https://all-naturalspirit.files.wordpress.com/2020/08/younger-futhark-icelandic-rune-poem-1.pdf) are available from my website to go along with the Deck.

WHAT ARE BINDRUNES?

Bindrunes are rune combination, which is speculated to be have been used for the initials of the carver's name (Figure 19). Bindrunes are generally 2 – 3 runes joined together to form a glyph (i.e., writing used to indicate a specific meaning) using a common vertical anchor point. They are common for the Anglo-Saxon Futhorc, but there are representatives for the Elder Futhark and Younger Futhark as well.

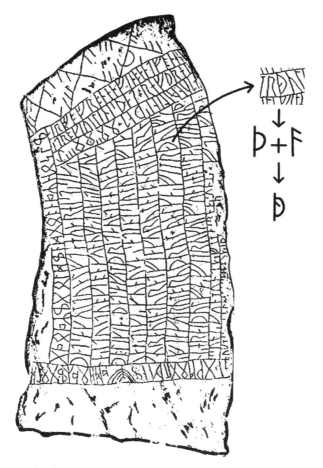

Figure 19: An example of a Younger Futhark bindrune from the sketched Rökstenen. The Þ and a symbols have been combined.

The creation of bindrunes is not limited to ancient inscriptions, many hobbyists and metaphysicians have also created their own set of bindrunes, specifically to combine the metaphysical properties of the runes. I have also created my own set of bindrunes!

LAST WORDS

My studies into the Elder Futhark, which have fascinated me since childhood, has been to gain knowledge from the quest of understanding the origins of the runes as well as recognizing the runes as a useful tool with which to pursue creative endeavors. I do not believe that the science and spirituality of the runes should be separated as these have both become incased in the identity of the runic alphabets. However, the integration of the science and the metaphysics requires a lot of discipline. From the purely spiritual or metaphysical side we must take care not to denote ignorance or speculation as the truth of the runes due to a lack of source material. Similarly, the purely materialistic side of academia does not improve the factual understanding of the runes and of ourselves by denying the metaphysical aspect of the runes and its potential contributions to the human psyche.

In this spirit; I have created my website (allnaturalspirit.com), written books, created rune art and oracle decks. I would invite you along the rest of my metaphysical journey into the runes whilst keeping a healthy dose of scientific discipline and interrogation to not take anything at face value. I am constantly on the lookout for new information, especially from the rare new research and historical references, regarding the runic alphabets, which I regularly integrate into the existing body of knowledge provided in these books.

Thus, please have a look at my 'Books in the Series' section and consider reading one of the follow-up in the series that piques your interest.

Thank you for reading my book and I always appreciate any feedback or reviews!

Happy Discovering!
All Natural Spirit

* * *

MOST INFORMATIVE REFERENCES

Reference List

1. Corsetti, A. (2020). *Putting the Elder Futhark into a Young Spiritualism: A Semantic Analysis of an Odinist Divination Guidebook.* Curiosity: Interdisciplinary Journal of Research and Innovation, 1 (1), p.12351.

2. Fulk, R.D. (2018). *A comparative grammar of the Early Germanic languages.* John Benjamins Publishing Company. 3. p. 11 - 26

3. Daniels, B. (2015) *Runes: Notes on Orthography and Pronunciation, as well as Some Thoughts on Using Runes to Write Modern English.* http://www.yokoiscool.com

4. Schulte, M. (2015) *Runology and historical sociolinguistics: On runic writing and its social history in the first millennium.* Journal of Historical Sociolinguistics. 1(1): 87-110.

5. Van Renterghem, A. (2014) *The Anglo-Saxon runic poem: a critical reassessment.* Masters Dissertation, University of Glasgow. pp. 113

6. Robertson, J. S. (2012) *How the Germanic Futhark Came from the*

Roman Alphabet Futhark. International Journal of Runic Studies 2: 7-25.

7. Oswald, B. (2008) *Discovering Runes*. Chartwell Books Inc.

8. Page, R. I. (2005) *Runes*, The British Museum Press, ISBN 0-7141-8065-3.

9. McKinnell, J., Simek R. and Düwel K. (2004) *Runes, Magic and Religion: a Sourcebook*. Wien: Fassbaender

10. Werner, C. G. (2004). *The allrunes Font and Package*. The Comprehensive Tex Archive Network.

11. Barnes, Michael P. (1998). *"The Transitional Inscriptions". In Beck, Heinrich; Düwel, Klaus. Runeninschriften als Quellen Interdisziplinärer Forschung*. Berlin: Walter de Gruyter. pp. 448–61. ISBN 3-11-015455-2. p. 451.

12. Page, R., I. (1987) *Reading The Past: Runes*. University of California Press.

* * *

ABOUT THE AUTHOR

All Natural Spirit

I am a pathfinder, always setting onto unknown roads and discovering new perspectives. The knowledge I gain through my ad-
ventures allows me to create new systems
and innovate existing ones. I am a pub-
lished scientist in the life sciences with several peer-reviewed academic journals. My

scientific mind lends the discipline and structure to pursue my
metaphysical projects. I am also a certified Crystal Healing Practitioner with the Sunshine Academy of Metaphysics. I created
All Natural Spirit as the public persona of my spiritual identity,
because as a scientist; I question the conservative and rigid think-
ing of modern day materialism and the close-minded dogma of
academia. All Natural Spirit (https://allnaturalspirit.com/) has
manifested as a website and blog where I regularly publish articles and even a series of free oracle cards. I believe in open-
source information as well as disseminating complex scholarly
or scientific studies to the public by making it more relatable to a
wider audience, hence the creation of my books and art.

BOOKS IN THIS SERIES

Runes

Celestial Rune Sigils: Elder Futhark Bindrunes

This is the first and only book (which I am aware of) that is exclusively dedicated to a comprehensive system of bind runes created from the Elder Futhark!

My studies into the Elder Futhark, which have fascinated me since childhood, have been converted into a coherent system of bindrunes for everyday use without the requirement of expert knowledge.

This bindrune project I have named the Celestial Rune Sigils. It started as a set of magickal tools with which to facilitate self-improvement through the exploration of spirituality. Subsequently, I have transformed the bindrunes into a set of 24 black and white sigils, representative of their origins from the 24 Elder Futhark Runes. The sigils were initially featured on the Celestial Rune Sigils oracle deck (more details on my website) and now they have been converted into book format as well! In this book I provide guidance on the crafting, uses and invocation of the Celestial Rune Sigils.

These sigils are not merely meant for use in divination, but rather they have a more active role with each sigil having a specific intention and contribution towards metaphysical, spiritual and magickal rituals. Therefore, the Celestial Rune Sigils are not only restricted to tarot readers or oracle enthusiasts. They have been created for the larger metaphysical community and would be of special interest to our energy workers and magick wielders. They are appropriate for most ages, including the very young and those who are wiser, since they can be used for both personal rituals and to assist clients during various healing and/or magick sessions.

The Celestial Rune Sigils represent a metaphysical, spiritual or magickal toolbox, with each sigil representing a different metaphysical tool. Each sigil can be used in this way, much as one would use a wand, crystal or other spiritual tool. There is a lot of freedom as to how precisely to apply each card and I hope that the practitioners who make use of this book will find their own intuitive ways of applying each of the sigils during their spiritual journeys and magickal rituals.

Elder Futhark Arcanum: An Intuitive Interpretation Of Rune Meanings

Are you an open-minded spiritual practitioner? A seeker of truth and knowledge? Someone who is willing to discuss alternate perspectives? Then this book is for you.
Here within is my attempt at finding the truth behind the purpose and origin of the Elder Futhark as well as intuitively deciphering their somewhat obscure meanings.

At a glance this book provides:
* Discussion on how runes became a language used for divination
* Modern meaning interpretations for each rune
* Abstract geometric artwork for each rune
* Additional western alchemical and astronomical associations for each rune
* Several overview tables and references

In this context, this book does not discuss the traditional meanings or interpretations of the runes, but rather more modern outlooks and perspectives on each. Instead of adding more content to already confusing and conflicting traditional/conventional meanings – I have opted for the opposite, to simplify rather than complicate. I have tried to distill the core of each rune through my studies into their history, linguistics and metaphysics in order to make clear delineations between the runes. Thus, brief mentions are made to traditional meanings in favour of more discussion around the transference of the runes into our daily lives with reference to more familiar circumstances and challenges.

I am quite partial to the metaphysical symbolism of animals, plants and objects, thus this book includes plenty representations form the animal kingdom as well as everyday objects and some minor contributions from herbology. I have tried to keep to the mythology related to the Germanic tribes and to the everyday references of people living in Iron Age Europe. Therefore, some of my interpretations are similar to their traditional counterparts, but the majority of them have been cast anew.

I truly appreciate any review and feedback as I am constantly striving towards improving this runic body of work!

Printed in Great Britain
by Amazon